VESPERTILIO

by Barry McStay

‖SAMUEL FRENCH‖

Copyright © 2021 by Barry McStay
All Rights Reserved

Vespertilio is fully protected under the copyright laws of the British Commonwealth, including Canada, the United States of America, and all other countries of the Copyright Union. All rights, including professional and amateur stage productions, recitation, lecturing, public reading, motion picture, radio broadcasting, television, online/digital production, and the rights of translation into foreign languages are strictly reserved.

ISBN 978-0-573-13259-9

concordtheatricals.co.uk

concordtheatricals.com

Cover artwork by Rebecca Pitt

FOR AMATEUR PRODUCTION ENQUIRIES

UNITED KINGDOM AND WORLD
EXCLUDING NORTH AMERICA
licensing@concordtheatricals.co.uk
020-7054-7200

Each title is subject to availability from Concord Theatricals, depending upon country of performance.

CAUTION: Professional and amateur producers are hereby warned that *Vespertilio* is subject to a licensing fee. The purchase, renting, lending or use of this book does not constitute a license to perform this title(s), which license must be obtained from the appropriate agent prior to any performance. Performance of this title(s) without a license is a violation of copyright law and may subject the producer and/or presenter of such performances to penalties. Both amateurs and professionals considering a production are strongly advised to apply to the appropriate agent before starting rehearsals, advertising, or booking a theatre. A licensing fee must be paid whether the title is presented for charity or gain and whether or not admission is charged.

This work is published by Samuel French, an imprint of Concord Theatricals. Ltd

The Professional Rights in this play are controlled by The Agency, 24 Pottery Lane, Notting Hill, London W11 4LZ.

No one shall make any changes in this title for the purpose of production. No part of this book may be reproduced, stored in a retrieval system, scanned, uploaded, or transmitted in any form, by any means, now known or yet to be invented, including mechanical, electronic, digital, photocopying, recording, videotaping, or otherwise, without the prior written permission of the publisher. No one shall share this title, or part of this title, to any social media or file hosting websites.

The moral right of Barry McStay to be identified as author of this work has been asserted in accordance with Section 77 of the Copyright, Designs and Patents Act 1988.

USE OF COPYRIGHTED MUSIC

A licence issued by Concord Theatricals to perform this play does not include permission to use the incidental music specified in this publication. In the United Kingdom: Where the place of performance is already licensed by the PERFORMING RIGHT SOCIETY (PRS) a return of the music used must be made to them. If the place of performance is not so licensed then application should be made to PRS for Music (www.prsformusic.com). A separate and additional licence from PHONOGRAPHIC PERFORMANCE LTD (www. ppluk.com) may be needed whenever commercial recordings are used. Outside the United Kingdom: Please contact the appropriate music licensing authority in your territory for the rights to any incidental music.

USE OF COPYRIGHTED THIRD-PARTY MATERIALS

Licensees are solely responsible for obtaining formal written permission from copyright owners to use copyrighted third-party materials (e.g., artworks, logos) in the performance of this play and are strongly cautioned to do so. If no such permission is obtained by the licensee, then the licensee must use only original materials that the licensee owns and controls. Licensees are solely responsible and liable for clearances of all third-party copyrighted materials, and shall indemnify the copyright owners of the play(s) and their licensing agent, Concord Theatricals Ltd., against any costs, expenses, losses and liabilities arising from the use of such copyrighted third-party materials by licensees.

IMPORTANT BILLING AND CREDIT REQUIREMENTS

If you have obtained performance rights to this title, please refer to your licensing agreement for important billing and credit requirements.

CAST AND CREATIVE

JOSHUA OAKES-ROGERS | JOSH
Joshua trained at the Royal Central School of Speech and Drama.
Theatre includes: *Vespertilio* (VAULT Festival and Dublin Fringe 2019); *Roseline* (Milan Tour 2018); *Lord Dismiss Us* (which received a nomination for Best Actor in a Supporting Role at the Offies – Edinburgh Fringe/Above the Stag 2017); *Body and Sold* (Park Theatre 2017); *Beauty On The Piste* (Above the Stag 2016).
Television includes: *The Dead Room* (BBC 2018); *Little Crackers: Harry Hill* (SKY1 2011).

BENEDICT SALTER | ALAN
Benedict trained at LAMDA.
Theatre credits include: *Lone Flyer* (Watermill Theatre); *A Christmas Carol* (Derby Theatre); *The Importance of Being Earnest* (Watermill Theatre); *Vespertilio* (VAULT Festival and Dublin Fringe); *Lady Windermere's Fan* (West End); *The Last Days of Anne Boleyn* (Tower of London); *A Little Night Music* (Watermill Theatre); *An Inspector Calls* (West End); *Shakespeare in Music* (RSC/ Southbank Sinfonia). Benedict was also a BBC Carleton Hobbs Bursary Award finalist in 2016.

BARRY MCSTAY | WRITER
Barry is an Irish writer and actor based in London. *Vespertilio* was his UK debut play when it opened in February 2019, winning a Show of the Week Award at VAULT Festival. It later ran at Smock Alley at the Dublin Fringe Festival in September 2019 before being filmed for streaming by the King's Head Theatre in April 2021.
His first play *Our Island* (dir. Maisie Lee, Project Arts Centre) ran at the Dublin Fringe Festival 2015 and was nominated for five Dublin Fringe Awards and a Writers Guild of Ireland Award.
Other work includes *Bir Tawil* (dir. Caitriona McLaughlin, Druid Theatre, 2017) and *The First* (dir. Emily Jenkins, VAULT Festival 2020). He has written short work for Miniaturists and the Abbey Theatre. In 2018, he was one of thirty writers selected to create a play for *A Play For Ireland* by Fishamble: The New Play Company. His writing has been longlisted for the Bruntwood Prize, the Theatre503 Playwriting Award and the Papatango Prize.
Barry has a BA (English Literature & History) from Trinity College Dublin and an MA (Acting) from East 15 Acting School.

LUCY JANE ATKINSON | DIRECTOR
Lucy is an experienced and award-winning director. Her work focuses on new writing, including musical theatre, devising, and immersive theatre. In 2018 she was named number 1 on The Stage's Top Talents To Watch, stating "her direction is simple, but acutely sensitive to the shifting energy of the writing. Evident but never overbearing."
Theatre credits include: *A Hundred Words For Snow* by Tatty Hennessy – VAULT Festival, UK tour, Trafalgar Studios (winner: Outstanding New Work, VAULT 2018; Winner: Off West-End Award for Best Actress; Nominated: Off West-End Awards for Best Director, Most Promising Playwright, and Best New Play), *Vespertilio* (VAULT Festival, Dublin Fringe; winner: Show of the Week VAULT 2019), and *MEAT*, by Gillian Greer, (Theatre503).
Her first filmed piece, *Testament*, by Tristan Bernays, was released in spring 2021.
She has directed work in Britain, the United States, and Canada, and is currently developing a further host of plays with an eclectic mix of some of the UK's most exciting up-and-coming playwrights.

JESS DUXBURY | PRODUCER
Jess has worked in theatre and live events since 2012. She produces theatre as well as virtual, digital and physical live events across the UK and Europe. She started out producing for comedy collective Casual Violence Comedy at the Edinburgh Fringe Festival and London venues, and went on to work with Dream Think Speak on their site-specific piece *Absent* at Shoreditch Town Hall. She produced *Vespertilio*'s inaugural production at the VAULT Festival in 2019 with Fight & Hope before helping it transfer to the Dublin Fringe Festival in September 2019.
She is passionate about female-led theatre and queer stories being given the space and the platform they deserve.
She has a BA (Hons) in English Literature and Drama from the University of Sussex.

VERITY JOHNSON | DESIGNER
Theatre includes as lead designer: *1984* (Nuffield Theatre Southampton); *Maggie May* (Finborough Theatre – Offie nominated for set design); *Vespertilio* (VAULT Festival); *How to Disappear Completely and Never Be Found* (Nuffield Theatre Southampton); *The Queen's Nose* (LSMT); *Bury The Dead* (Finborough Theatre); *Unexpected Joy* (Southwark Playhouse); *Half Me Half You* (Wild Project, NYC); *Mermaids* (King's Head Theatre); *Nine Foot Nine* (Bunker Theatre); *Hilda and Virginia* (Jermyn Street Theatre); *Testament* (VAULT Festival); *The House of Usher* (The Hope Theatre); *The Dumb Waiter* (Maltings Arts Theatre). As an assistant *Hamlet* and *As You Like It* (Shakespeare's Globe);

The Audience (NST City); *Rotterdam* (The Arts Theatre); *German Skerries* (Orange Tree Theatre); *Microcosm* (Soho Theatre).
Verity trained at Wimbledon College of Art.

ZIA BERGIN-HOLLY | LIGHTING DESIGNER
Lighting designs for Theatre include: *Two* (HullTruck Theatre); *Flights* (One Duck Theatre); *MEAT* (Theatre503); *Promises Promises* (Centrál Színház Budapest); *Cleft, Melt* (Rough Magic); *Top Hat* (Silver Blue Entertainment); *Bread Not Profits* (Gúna Nua); *Apologia, The Lion in Winter* and *Hand to God* (The English Theatre Frankfurt); *Frankie and Johnny* in The Clair De Lune (Northern Stage); *Annie* (Cork Opera House); *The Nest* (Lyric Theatre Belfast and Young Vic Theatre London); *The Importance Of Nothing* (Pan Pan) for which Zia won Best Lighting Design at The Irish Times Theatre Awards and *FABRIC* (Robin Rayner Productions) which won a Scotsman Fringe First Award.
Set and Lighting designs for Theatre include: *EMBARGO* (Fishamble); *Solar Bones* (Rough Magic and Kilkenny Arts Festival); *The Misfits* (Corn Exchange); *User Not Found* (Dante or Die); *They Called Her Vivaldi* (Theatre Lovett).
She also designed the set for the Olympia Theatre, Dublin performances of Grace Jones concerts for Bloodlight and Bami by Blinder Films.

ANNIE MAY FLETCHER | SOUND DESIGNER
Annie trained at LAMDA and was the Lab Associate Sound Designer at Nuffield Southampton Theatres in 2018/19. She is currently an Associate Artist with Snapper Theatre and is a runner up in the Evening Standard's Future Theatre Fund 2021 in the Audio Design category.
Theatre credits include: *The Understudy Live* (Palace Theatre); *MEAT* and *The Amber Trap* (Theatre503); *Humbug! The Hedgehog Who Couldn't Sleep* (The Albany, NST City); *In My Lungs The Ocean Swells* (VAULT Festival); *Ad Libido* (Soho Theatre, UK Tour); *Fledlings, 1984* and *How To Disappear Completely and Never Be Found* (NST City) and *The Importance of Being Earnest* (Bolton Octagon).
Associate credits include: *Enough* (Traverse Theatre); *HOW NOT TO DROWN* (Glasgow Tron, Lawrence Batley Theatre); *The Audience* (NST City); *Acceptance* (Hampstead Theatre) and *100 Words For Snow* (Trafalgar Studios, VAULT Festival).
Digital credits include: *Oh Woman!* (Manchester Royal Exchange); *A Passion Play* (45North); *Luna The Jaguar* (Greenpeace UK); *TOAST* (Lawrence Batley Theatre) and *The Understudy* (Lawrence Batley Theatre).
www.anniemayfletcher.co.uk

KING'S HEAD THEATRE
ESTD 1970

The King's Head Theatre was established in 1970. Passionate about championing ethically produced fringe theatre, we are known for our challenging work and support of young artists.

In 2019, 88,029 audience members saw a show of ours: 37,586 at our 110-seater home on Upper Street and 50,443 elsewhere. At our home in Islington we had 686 performances last year of 113 different shows.

We are committed to fighting prejudice through the work we stage, the artists and staff we work with and by producing work for minority audience groups. We believe in fair pay for all on the fringe and create accessible routes for early career artists to stage their work; work we are passionate about.

In 2017, we announced the theatre is on the move. Subject to a fundraising campaign, the King's Head Theatre will move into a custom-built space in the heart of Islington Square, directly behind its current home securing the future of the venue for generations to come.

115 Upper Street, London, N1 1QN
kingsheadtheatre.com

SUPPORT THE KING'S HEAD THEATRE

"The King's Head Theatre is a genuine community space. It's part of the lifeblood of Upper Street and a hub for actors, directors and stage managers."
Mark Gatiss

The King's Head Theatre is an ambitious, thriving producing house located in the heart of Islington. From the emerging companies and creatives, to the thousands of audience members we welcome through our doors every year, people are at the heart of everything we do.

Famous for an unapologetically broad programme of work and an unwavering commitment to ethical employment on the fringe, the King's Head Theatre occupies a unique place in the capital's theatre ecology.

Each year, the King's Head Theatre needs to raise £100,000 to keep producing and presenting ambitious work that supports, develops and values our artists, staff, audiences and alumni. We hope you will join us on that journey by becoming one of our Supporters.

For further information visit **www.kingsheadtheatre.com** or to discuss bespoke packages, please contact us on
info@kingsheadtheatre.com

King's Head Theatre is a registered charity Charity No: 1161483

KEY TO THE STAGE DOOR from £150 per year
Priority booking period
Exchange and reserve tickets at no extra cost
KHT Insights email with news and announcements Invitation to supporters night
Acknowledgement in our published programmes
£310 pays an actor's wages for one week

KEY TO THE DRESSING ROOM from £500 per year
Key to the Stage Door membership benefits plus:
Invitation to annual 'Behind the Scenes Breakfast' to hear the Artistic Director share upcoming plans
Personal booking via the office
£500 pays for the costumes for one opera

KEY TO THE KING'S HEAD from £1,000 per year
Key to the Dressing Room membership benefits plus:
Invitation to breakfast with the Executive Director Opportunity to book house seats to sold out shows
£1,375 supports the Director for one show

ARTISTIC DIRECTOR'S CIRCLE from £2,500 per year
Key to the King's Head membership benefits plus:
Signed playtext for each production attended
Invitation to lunch with the Artistic Director once a year A backstage tour of the theatre for you and up to 5 guests finishing with drinks on our stage
£2,500 pays for set design for one play

AMBASSADOR from £5,000 per year
All of the benefits of Artistic Director's Circle plus:
Invitations to our Press Nights and post-show parties and the chance to create additional bespoke benefits suited to your interests
£5,775 pays for actors throughout rehearsals

KING'S HEAD THEATRE

Executive Director	Fiona English
Interim Programme Director *	Heather Ruck
Producer	Michelle Barnette
Marketing Manager	Oscar French
Box Office Manager	Alan Stratford
Theatre Manager *	Richard Lambert
Development Manager	Mabs Rahman
Finance Manager *	Katherine De Halpert
Assistant Producer	Rohan Perumatantri
Assistant Theatre Manager	Christina Gazelidis
Marketing Officer	Shaadi Khosravi-Rad
Box Office Assistants*	Hannah Collins
	Alexander Hick
	Dominic Listori
	Katie Mcleod
	Charlie Norburn
	Germma Orleans-Thompson
Trainee Resident Directors ^	Amber Sinclair-Case
	Matt Strachan
	Monty Leigh
	Ella Murdoch
Trustees ^	Kate Farrell
	Mary Lauder
	Amanda Mascarenhas
	Amanda Moulson
	James Seabright (Chair)
	Molly Waiting
	Richard Williamson

* Part Time ^ Voluntary

The King's Head Theatre is 51 years old, here are just a few of the highlights of our journey so far...

1970   Dan Crawford founds the first pub theatre in London for over 400 years and the King's Head Theatre is born.

1982   Mr Cinders, starring Joanna Lumley, opens, before transferring to the West End for 527 performances.

1983   Victoria Wood's first solo stand-up show, Lucky Bag, opens to rave reviews.

1988   Premier of Tom Stoppard's Artist Descending a Staircase opens before transferring to Broadway.

1991   Steven Berkoff directs and stars in the UK premiere of Kvetch at the King's Head Theatre.

2002   Trainee Resident Directors Scheme wins Royal Anniversary Trust Award.

2010   OperaUpClose becomes a resident company.

2011   La bohème wins the Olivier Award for Best New Opera.

2015   Trainspotting is first performed at the King's Head Theatre – it has since had more than 1000 performances all over the world.

2016   43,857 audience members see a show at our London home - our highest footfall ever.

2017   La bohème & Strangers in Between transfer Trafalgar Studios 2 in London's West End.

2019   Kevin Elyot's Coming Clean and Opera Undone transfer to Trafalgar Studios 2 in London's West End.

2022   Subject to a successful fundraising campaign, we move to our permanent new home in Islington Square.

THANKS

Barry would like to thank Patrick Barkham, Dr Joe Nunez-Mino and The Bat Conservation Trust, Jenny Clark OBE, Tony Hutson. Tristan Bernays, Bob Duxbury and Joan Frank, Annie and Gary Duxbury, Seana Mallen and Richard Atkinson, Terry Mallen, Mark McStay, Cristina Thorson. LAMDA, Italia Conti and the Abbey Theatre set departments. Liz Isles. Ian Bonar, Trieve Blackwood-Cambridge and Richard Lounds. Gill Greer, Becky Brown, Bríd Kirby, Mat Burtcher, Andy George and VAULT Festival. Ruth McGowan, Smock Alley Theatre and the Dublin Fringe Festival. Michelle Barnette and the King's Head Theatre. Charlie Coulthard. Nick Quinn and Maeve Bolger for looking after me. Jess and Lizzie for making it happen. Verity, Zia, Annie, Amie, Frances, Madison and Hanan for giving pictures to the words. Benedict and Joshua for making my heart swell and break. Mum and Dad for everything and more. Mikey for all the heartbeats. And Lucy for going for a walk on Primrose Hill, for singing "The Bat Song" and for your generosity of genius. You are amazing.

VESPERTILIO received its world premiere on 20th February 2019 in The Cavern at the VAULT Festival, Waterloo, London. Written by Barry McStay, Director Lucy Jane Atkinson, Producer Jess Duxbury, Designer Verity Johnson, Lighting Designer Zia Bergin-Holly, Sound Designer Annie May Fletcher, Assistant Director Amie Burns-Walker, Stage Manager Frances White. Original artwork Madison Coby. The cast was as follows:

ALAN . . . . Benedict Salter
JOSH . . . . Joshua Oakes-Rogers
RADIO VOICES . . . . Victoria Cook, Toby Manley,
Rhiannon Neads and Andrew McDonald

VESPERTILIO was performed at Dublin Fringe Festival (Smock Alley – the Boys School), 17th–22nd September 2019. Produced by Jess Duxbury & Elizabeth Benbow (Fight and Hope), Director Lucy Jane Atkinson, Producer Jess Duxbury, Designer Verity Johnson, Lighting Designer Zia Bergin-Holly, Sound Designer Annie May Fletcher, Stage Manager Frances White. The cast was as follows:

ALAN . . . . Benedict Salter
JOSH . . . . Joshua Oakes-Rogers
RADIO VOICES . . . . Victoria Cook, Toby Manley,
Rhiannon Neads and Andrew McDonald

This production of *VESPERTILIO* was recorded at the King's Head Theatre and was available to watch on the venue's website from Thursday 15 April to Wednesday 12 May 2021. Filmed by Shoot Media and streamed by Kings Head Theatre as part of Plays On Film. Produced by Jess Duxbury (Fight and Hope), Director Lucy Jane Atkinson, Set Designer Verity Johnson, Lighting Designer Zia Bergin-Holly, Sound Designer Annie May Fletcher, Artwork Designer Rebecca Pitt. The cast was as follows:

ALAN . . . . Benedict Salter
JOSH . . . . Joshua Oakes-Rogers
RADIO VOICES . . . . Victoria Cook, Toby Manley,
Rhiannon Neads and Mikey Brett

CHARACTERS

ALAN – 39ish
JOSH – 19ish
RADIO VOICES

AUTHOR'S NOTES

Vespertilio was inspired by an article in *The Guardian* newspaper by Patrick Barkham, *"*The last bat: the mystery of Britain's most solitary animal*"* (12th June 2018). If possible, the opening scene should be lit by Alan's torchlight alone.

CONTENT WARNING

Contains very strong language, scenes of a sexual nature, references to homophobic abuse, bullying, suicide and homelessness.

NOTE ON THE TEXT

Line breaks within speech are intended to indicate the characters speech and thought patterns. A dash – is used to indicate hesitation, interruption, change of mind or the unsaid. A slash / is used to indicate overlapping lines. Lines without / may still overlap.

(An abandoned railway tunnel near Chichester.)

(A torch flares on.)

JOSH. Fuck!

ALAN. Jesus!

JOSH. Fuck!

ALAN. Who's there?!

JOSH. Fuck man!

ALAN. Stay there!

JOSH. Fucking hell –

ALAN. Stop!

JOSH. Stop shining that / in my –

ALAN. / Hands up!

JOSH. Hands up!?

ALAN. Shhhh!

JOSH. Hands up?!

ALAN. Shhhhhhhhhh!

JOSH. Hands up?!

ALAN. Shhhhhh!!

JOSH. You don't / even –

ALAN. / Keep it / down –

JOSH. / You ain't got a / gun mate!

ALAN. / I know! Just hush!

JOSH. Hush?

ALAN. Shhhhh!

JOSH. Why!?

ALAN. Bloody hell, be quiet!

JOSH. Fucking scared the / shit outta –

ALAN. / Who are you?

JOSH. Who the fuck are / YOU?

ALAN. / What are you doing / here?

JOSH. / What are YOU doing / here?

ALAN. / You shouldn't be here!

JOSH. Should you?

ALAN. Yes.

JOSH. Yeah?

ALAN. How did you get in?

JOSH. What?

ALAN. You broke in.

JOSH. No?

ALAN. Picked the lock did you?

JOSH. What?

ALAN. I told / them –

JOSH. / I didn't pick any / locks –

ALAN . / The path is too clear, / it's way too obvious –

JOSH. / You're fucking crazy, / bruv –

ALAN. / You shouldn't be here –

JOSH. Why?

ALAN. You need to leave –

JOSH. Fucking –

ALAN. Come peacefully / or –

JOSH. / Come / peacefully?!

ALAN. / I'll be forced / to –

JOSH. / Don't touch me, mate!

ALAN. I don't want things to get violent –

JOSH. Who's getting violent?!

ALAN. I'm making a citizen's arrest!

JOSH. Who are you!?

ALAN. You have a right to remain / silent –

JOSH. / Hahaha / ha –

ALAN. / But anything you do say / will be –

JOSH. / Hahahahahahahaha / haha –

ALAN. / Used against – what? Why are you –

Be quiet, for heaven's sake!

JOSH. Hahahahaha – sorry.

Sorry sorry shhh sorry.

Hahahaha.

ALAN. Shhh.

JOSH. Shhhhhh! Yes, shhhh!

Ha.

Man – where are you, like what planet are you from?

ALAN. I don't know / what –

JOSH. / Is this your first time speaking English?

ALAN. You really must leave.

JOSH. Says who, bruv?

ALAN. For the final time, be quiet!

JOSH. What's the problem?

ALAN. Them.

JOSH. Who?

ALAN. The bats.

JOSH. What?

ALAN. Bats.

JOSH. Shit man, bats!?

ALAN. Shut up!

JOSH. There are bats here!?

ALAN. Calm down.

JOSH. That's fucking cool – where?

ALAN. There.

(All over the roof of the tunnel.)

JOSH. Shit man, that's wicked.

Shit – there's fucking tonnes of them.

ALAN. Exactly –

JOSH. That's fucking cool – my friend Lee has snakes and lizards and stuff, I love weird pets and shit like that –

ALAN. They're not pets –

JOSH. No, right –

ALAN. This is their hibernation roost.

JOSH. Oh right –

ALAN. You're disturbing them.

JOSH. There's tonnes of 'em, how many are there –

ALAN. Tonnes, can you please leave?

JOSH. Why are you here then?

ALAN. Are you listening?

JOSH. No – why won't you answer me?

ALAN. Because you're a stranger and you shouldn't be here.

JOSH. Well far as I know, you're a stranger and you shouldn't be here.

ALAN. I should.

JOSH. Says you.

So. We're stuck. Aren't we?

–

Shall we start again? Hi, I'm Josh.

ALAN. Please go.

JOSH. What's your name?

ALAN. Go.

JOSH. Do you come here often?

ALAN. Go!

JOSH. Shhh! You'll wake the bats.

ALAN. I'm going to call the police.

JOSH. Mate, chill out. What's your name?

For fuck's sake, I'm not gonna attack you or anything, just be a normal human being, right?

I'm Josh.

ALAN. Alan Stafford.

JOSH. Nice to meet you, Alan Stafford.

See, not so bad is it?

ALAN. How did you get in?

JOSH. The drain down the end, it was hanging open –

ALAN. I told them – it's been rusting through –

JOSH. Is it your tunnel then, like do you own the land or something?

ALAN. No.

JOSH. Right.

Listen, I'm sorry. I didn't know about the bats did I? I just needed a place to sleep. For a few nights.

Okay?

ALAN. Oh. Right.

I didn't –

–

I'm sorry. To hear that.

Sorry.

But isn't there – is there not somewhere else – you could – a bit nicer –?

JOSH. No.

Good enough for the bats, innit? Good enough for me.

So you're their – what? Zookeeper?

ALAN. I monitor them.

JOSH. Right. Monitor. The bat guy.

–

You're Batman!

ALAN. Please don't.

JOSH. That makes you Batman!

ALAN. Really –

JOSH. You're a superhero!

ALAN. It's not very original –

JOSH. *(Bale Batman voice.)* 'There's a storm coming –'

ALAN. Please –

JOSH. *(Ledger Joker voice.)* 'Why so serious?'

ALAN. I'd really prefer it if you stopped, alright?

    (Silence.)

Look. I'm sorry but –

disturbing bats mid-hibernation can kill them – and several are highly endangered –

well, there's one in particular –

he's the only one left. And I don't want to –

I'm sorry – you can't stay here.

I can – I can call someone for you. If you need. What about your parents or –? A hostel or –

JOSH. I've got my own phone, mate.

ALAN. I feel awful –

JOSH. Yeah. Well.

If I was a bat –

ALAN. Come on –

JOSH. Yeah yeah yeah –

ALAN. I really hope you understand.

JOSH. I don't. But you don't either, so it's cool.

ALAN. He's unique.

JOSH. So am I.

    (Exits.)

(A civic hall.)

ALAN. Bats are amazing. *Chiroptera* are cool. And I'm going to tell you why.

They're the only mammal that can fly. There's over twelve hundred species worldwide – actually, one in five species of mammal is a bat. They've been around for a long time – the oldest bat fossil is fifty two million years old. They pollinate flowers – hashtag Not Just Bees. They have huge variety – from the tiny pipistrelle which weights less than a pound coin, to the huge flying foxes of Java, with a wing span of two metres – they're remarkable.

Let me tell you a story. The hero of this story is the greater mouse-eared bat.

Yes, there is also a lesser mouse-eared bat. I'll actually take questions at the end, if that's alright. The greater mouse-eared bat is part of a family called the *vespertilionidae* or evening bats. The Latin for bat is *vespertilio*. There's a bit of Latin in this, sorry. The official species name for the greater mouse-eared bat is *myotis myotis*. *Myotis myotis* has been extinct in Britain since 1992.

Yes. They're widespread across Europe but we managed to wipe them out, the first mammal we drove to extinction in this country since the wolf, in the seventeen hundreds. Well done us.

The greater-mouse eared bat became a celebrity when it first appeared in Britain. In 1957, a colony was discovered in an old mine on the Isle of Purbeck, down in Dorset. And the country went bats for bats. Ahem. *The Times* published photographs, collectors stole them, rewards were offered for dead ones, TV programmes came and took them out of hibernation to put them on telly.

It was the Fifties, there wasn't much else to do.

So that colony didn't return. And they were completely gone from the UK by the early nineties. All sorts of things have helped drive down the bat population – insecticides, too many bright lights, wind turbines, even things like the new section of the A27, near here, the bit they're about to build – it'll disrupt hunting and migration routes.

But that's not the end of the story.

In 2002, a single male was found in an abandoned railway tunnel near Chichester. He was barely a year old at the time. Every winter since then he has hibernated, about three hundred metres inside this dark damp tunnel for nearly five months. It's perfect for our heroic greater mouse-eared bat .

He safely spends the winter months there, among many other hibernating bats.

And then he disappears every spring – we don't know where. We've never seen him in flight. We've never made the location of the tunnel public – we don't want a repeat of 1957.

We carefully inspected the greater mouse-eared bat while he hibernated in 2007 and found that his private parts have never been sexually active. Chances are he will spend the rest of his life alone. But that doesn't make him, in any sense, a loser. In my eyes, and hopefully in yours too, he's a winner. Durable. Indefatigable. Triumphant. A real survivor.

After all, that's the goal. The whole point of things. To survive.

(After the speech.)

JOSH. That was good.

ALAN. What?

JOSH. Really good.

ALAN. Why are you here?

JOSH. Are you gonna ask me that every time we meet –

ALAN. What are you doing?

JOSH. I wanted to see your speech.

ALAN. How did –

JOSH. I googled your name, Alan Stafford. Some bat fancier's message board came up, someone was saying "oh, Alan Stafford is giving a talk tonight, can't wait, he's so dreamy" et cetera – you've got a following, mate. People stanning for you hard online –

ALAN. I don't know what that means –

JOSH. You're a bat celeb. The Justin Bieber of the bat world –

ALAN. I don't know who that is.

JOSH. Yes you do.

ALAN. I know of him.

JOSH. How old are you, like eighty?

ALAN. I'm thirty-nine –

JOSH. Even my nan knows who he is –

ALAN. Did you find somewhere to stay?

JOSH. Sure.

ALAN. Where?

JOSH. Is this bat really the only one then?

ALAN. Josh –

JOSH. And he's never had sex?

ALAN. Josh –

JOSH. Cos that must suck.

ALAN. Please –

JOSH. Lucky he has you to look after him –

ALAN. Where did you –

JOSH. In a fucking field under a trailer, alright?

–

I didn't go back to the tunnel. Alright?

And after hearing you talk, I'm glad I didn't disturb anything.

It's a good story. You're a good man. Well done.

ALAN. Wait.

JOSH. Yes?

–

I don't want your pity.

ALAN. Okay.

I'm sorry.

JOSH. You were frightened. You were just protecting him.

ALAN. Still –

JOSH. It's alright. I understand. You have to protect the things that matter. I get it. And you look good. Up there, in full flight. Wings spread! I like people who care about stuff. It's good to give a shit.

ALAN. That sounds like it should be on a poster.

JOSH. Or a meme.

ALAN. What's a meme?

JOSH. I can't tell if you're joking or not.

ALAN. I don't really do jokes.

JOSH. Is that a joke?

ALAN. You're very confident.

JOSH. Charming even.

Your mouth.

ALAN. What?

JOSH. It's – ha. I've just noticed. I've never seen that.

ALAN. What?

JOSH. It turns down at one end and up at the other.

ALAN. Does it?

JOSH. Has no one ever pointed it out?

ALAN. No?

JOSH. It does.

This end is a smile and this end is a frown.

Like it can't make up its mind.

ALAN. I hadn't – noticed.

JOSH. It's cute.

Bae got curves.

ALAN. Um. Thank you.

I should probably be – you know?

JOSH. Meeting your fans.

ALAN. Well. There are some other members of the Bat Conservation Trust in and –

JOSH. But you'd rather talk to me.

ALAN. Would I?

JOSH. You're intrigued that I'm here.

ALAN. I'm more suspicious.

JOSH. So why are you still here?

ALAN. Gosh, you're exhausting.

JOSH. Yeah but you like me more than you're gonna admit. And you wouldn't mind buying me a drink. But you're a bit too scared to ask me. Which is fine because, lucky for you, I'm the sort of guy who will do the asking and answering for you. Yes, I'll have a drink with you – you're buying – mine's a lager.

ALAN. I'm not sure.

JOSH. Yes you are.

(**ALAN**'s *house. Crumbling and overcrowded with things.*)

ALAN. Mind your step. Sorry about all the – stuff, and stuff.

JOSH. Whoops!

ALAN. Careful!

JOSH. That shouldn't be – shouldn't be there –

ALAN. No yes, I should move it, or put up a sign or –

JOSH. A sign!? Ha!

ALAN. No no, not, that's silly – haha!

JOSH. This place is sick!

ALAN. That's a good thing, right?

JOSH. It's like Hogwarts or Narnia or something!

ALAN. You mean it's old.

JOSH. Yeah it's old but – I mean I like old things! Ha!

ALAN. Hey!

JOSH. There's so much STUFF!

ALAN. A life – lots of lives.

JOSH. This is all yours.

ALAN. I don't like throwing things out –

JOSH. Yeah, that's called hoarding, they could film – wassitcalled – "Storage Wars" in here, you know? Yeah, I know you don't know what that is.

ALAN. No. Haha.

JOSH. You live alone?

ALAN. I don't think anyone could – I'm very particular.

JOSH. Fuck that bollocks, we're all particular.

ALAN. I'm particularly particular –

JOSH. Well so am I.

ALAN. You're very particular.

JOSH. I am!

ALAN. I haven't had to live with anyone for more than a decade now. Since my father died.

JOSH. Oh I'm sorry – I'm sorry man –

ALAN. It's alright, it was a while ago –

JOSH. Yeah. But – you know – he's your dad. And –

yeah. Here.

(Hug.)

ALAN. I'm sorry, I never even offered you water – or tea or –

JOSH. Do we not have anything stronger?

ALAN. I don't really usually keep any alcohol in the house, to be honest. There might be some wine but it'll be just what I use for cooking or –

JOSH. What about a smoke?

ALAN. I don't like cigarettes.

JOSH. Not cigarettes.

ALAN. Oh. No. Right. No I don't do, don't do that either.

JOSH. Not even when you're tipsy?

ALAN. I'm not tipsy.

JOSH. You are! You're wobbling!

ALAN. I am not!

JOSH. You are too! Stand on one leg!

ALAN. I don't have to do anything – you're not the police!

JOSH. I'm making a citizen's arrest! Hahaha!

ALAN. Ha. I didn't know what I was saying, I was scared.

JOSH. Boo. I'm scary.

ALAN. Finding a strange man in the dark is a scary thing.

JOSH. A bit romantic too.

ALAN. In a tunnel covered in bat poo?

JOSH. Grosssssss.

ALAN. Why were you there?

JOSH. Does that matter?

My parents kicked me out.

ALAN. Well.

Gosh. I don't really know what to –

what to say.

JOSH. Normal human interaction is fine, Alan.

ALAN. Okay.

–

I'm sorry.

JOSH. Let's play a game.

ALAN. Aren't you tired?

JOSH. No! Never! Game!

ALAN. What do you want to play?

JOSH. What game would a bat play?

ALAN. I don't think there's many games bats could –

JOSH. Marco Polo!

ALAN. What?

JOSH. You don't know what Marco Polo is!

ALAN. Italian explorer, went to China –

JOSH. Noooooo fuck off mate, you know the game Marco Polo!

Marco! Polo! Marco! Polo! You know? So you can figure out where they are – like bats do –

ALAN. Oh, like echolocation!

JOSH. Echolocation yes that's the thing, that's what I, yes! I'll be the bat, and you be the – what? What do bats look for?

ALAN. Crickets.

JOSH. You really know how to get a bat all horny, don't you Alan?

ALAN. Or a beetle?

JOSH. Cricket is fine.

When I say cricket, you say bat, cricket – oh!

Hahaha –

ALAN. Oh cricket bat! Hahahaha –

JOSH. That was a total accident! Ha!

ALAN. Coincidences are wonderful.

JOSH. Yes they are.

Right.

Cricket!

ALAN. Bat.

JOSH. Cricket!

ALAN. Bat.

JOSH. Cricket!

ALAN. Bat.

JOSH. Cricket!

ALAN. Bat.

>(**ALAN** *initially tries to evade.*)

>(*Eventually tries to be caught.*)

>(**JOSH** *is stumbly, enthusiastic and competitive.*)

>(*And eventually, cheats.*)

JOSH. Cricket!

ALAN. Bat! Hey, you peeked!

JOSH. I wanted to catch you.

ALAN. You caught me.

>(*Some breaths.*)

JOSH. Hey.

ALAN. What?

JOSH. Your mouth.

ALAN. What?

JOSH. It just made up its mind.

>(*Kiss.*)

NEWSREADER. The leader of the Chichester District Council, Bob Langley, welcomed the final approval of the new section of the A27. The seven kilometre stretch of dual carriageway will cost in excess of seventy million pounds. But Mr Langley is satisfied this represents value for money.

BOB LANGLEY. This is a much-needed investment from the government and Highways England. Chichester residents are finally getting the infrastructure they truly need. It is real, definitive progress.

(*Post-shag.*)

JOSH. Welllllll –

ALAN. What?

JOSH. You're very good in bed.

ALAN. Thank you.

JOSH. "And so are you Josh".

ALAN. Sorry – yes, and so are you. Sorry – I'm not usually – Sorry.

JOSH. You don't have to say it if you don't think I am.

ALAN. You are. Very.

JOSH. You're not gonna get weird on me now?

ALAN. No.

JOSH. Or weirder.

ALAN. No.

JOSH. I'm not your first, am I?

ALAN. What?

JOSH. Your first time. Am I?!

ALAN. Oh god, no. Not my first.

No one with an iPhone is a virgin.

JOSH. Exactly.

I didn't think you were.

You suck like a pro.

Best I've had in a while.

–

Oh! I just remembered!

ALAN. What?

JOSH. The Bat Song!

ALAN. What bat song?

JOSH. The Bat Song! There's a bat song!

ALAN. Is there?

JOSH. Yes! I can't believe you don't know it, Mr Bat Alan!

ALAN. I don't know everything.

JOSH. Well you should. We learned it at Jesus Camp.

–

Summer camp but, y'know, with more God than kayaking. Actually we did kayaking too, while singing hymns – it was weird. My parents sent me.

Anyway. Listen.

(He sings the opening lines of a song in the style of the Banana Slug String Band **["BATS EAT BUGS"]***. *He's a decent singer. Alan doesn't applaud.)*

–

–

So. Yeah. There you go. The Bat Song.

ALAN. Not all bats eat bugs. Some are frugivorous. Or sanguivorous.

They eat fruit or blood.

---

* A licence to produce VESPERTILIO does not include a performance licence for "BATS EAT BUGS". The publisher and author suggest that the licensee contact PRS to ascertain the music publisher and contact such music publisher to license or acquire permission for performance of the song. If a licence or permission is unattainable for "BATS EAT BUGS", the licensee may not use the song in VESPERTILIO but should create an original composition in a similar style or use a similar song in the public domain. For further information, please see Music Use Note on page iii.

JOSH. Right.

I mean, it's just a song sooooooo chill?

ALAN. It's important to get things right. Factually.

JOSH. Alright.

–

So, how did you get into the bats thing?

ALAN. Sorry. I just –

I'm not used to people staying. And wanting to – talk.

I don't really talk. After – sex. And I don't – we don't know each other –

JOSH – We could.

ALAN. I'd – just now – tonight was just –

you know? One night.

JOSH. I'll go.

ALAN. No no no – you don't have to. It's late. And I don't want you – out there. Just – would you mind – sleeping in the spare room?

Please.

Sorry.

That's just how – it has to be.

It'll be easier for you to leave in the morning.

JOSH. Right.

–

So I'm leaving in the morning?

ALAN. I think so.

Yes. I think it would be best.

Please, stay. For now I mean. But not here.

JOSH. You're –

–

Man, you're a mystery. Do you just like kicking me out of places?

ALAN. Not at all – I'm sorry –

JOSH. It's cool. Apparently it's my thing.

ALAN. Josh –

JOSH. Down the hall is it? – never mind, I'll find it – don't let the bed bugs bite.

*(The morning after. **JOSH** holding **ALAN**'s wallet.)*

ALAN. What are you doing?

JOSH. You're awake.

ALAN. Are you –

JOSH. I made you breakfast –

ALAN. Put that down!

JOSH. What?

ALAN. Give it to me.

JOSH. Right.

Yeah. You think I'm stealing it?

Fucking hell, bruv, you really don't trust me, do you?

ALAN. Why should I? Give me my wallet.

JOSH. I was putting it back.

I wanted to make breakfast but your fridge was empty.

I don't have any money. I wanted to do – something – I borrowed it and went to the shop. Sorry.

Thought that counts, innit?

ALAN. – Yes.

Alright.

Thank you.

*(**JOSH**'s phone beeps. He looks – and ignores.)*

JOSH. I brought your post too.

ALAN. Thanks.

You're still here.

JOSH. Yeah. Sorry. I can get going – I just need a shower and –

ALAN. No no – it's – usually – people don't make breakfast. They don't bring your post. They don't stay.

JOSH. Sorry.

ALAN. I just thought – you'd want to – you wouldn't have to see me, or say goodbye.

JOSH. Well.

I don't have anywhere to – you know?

ALAN. Where are you from?

JOSH. Crawley. My dad's a pastor – he's got a small church, mum works in a charity shop. They're good people but – man, they're hard work. High standards for EVERYTHING. And everything was to, for, by the grace of God and –

sorry. It's so – fucking – fucked.

I can hear him saying "don't swear!" – huh huh!

I worked my arse off to get to a good uni like my brother. He's smart, straight A's, off to study law in Durham. And I got into general studies in Kent. He's clever. I'm just – average.

ALAN. You're certainly not average.

JOSH. Heyyyy! He does charming!

At least, uni was an achievement, something I could be proud of. So I went.

And I fell in love.

With a boy.

And I told them. And they kicked me out.

–

That's basically it.

ALAN. That's – awful.

JOSH. Yes.

> (**JOSH**'s *phone beeps. He looks – and ignores.*)

ALAN. I don't know what to say.

JOSH. You don't have to say anything. You gonna open your post?

ALAN. In a minute.

JOSH. That one looks important.

ALAN. Just a bill.

JOSH. "Urgent".

ALAN. It can wait.

–

Who was he? The boy.

JOSH. Oh. The most beautiful, kind guy. Obviously. Of course he fucking was.

As soon as I saw him I was just – I mean, I'd slept with plenty of guys – no one with an iPhone is a virgin! But it was all very on the DL and I felt all this shame after it. I was a mess inside. But when I got to uni I thought, right, new start, new leaf.

And I met him in my first week, in the student bar. With someone from my course, she knew him from their home town. And he shook my hand in the most confident way you've ever seen – like he was president of somewhere, right?

And I fucking – just – "take me now!" And we hung out that day and he took me back to his halls and we spent the weekend together and so on and so on and –

He was everything. Tall, dark, handsome, great in bed – massive dick – smart – and the way he looked –

right into my eyes – I mean, you can't blame me for falling in love.

ALAN. No.

JOSH. But they did anyway.

–

I was going to tell them over Christmas. I waited until the day before I had to go back to uni. And I sat down in the kitchen, and my brother was there too cos I thought if I tell them and it goes a bit wrong, he'll back me up, he's open-minded and stuff.

So. Yeah. "I've met a boy, I love him, I'm gay" –

fuck me man, that was the longest fucking silence of my life.

And then my dad goes "no you're not". And my mum goes "no you're not". And I looked at my brother – and he's just shaking his head.

I tried to get them to understand and they went from denial to trying to cure me – CURE me! – I was a sinful boy! And I kept shouting "What about love thy neighbour!?" Throwing their faith back in their faces.

My dad held the front door open and just said "get out" over and over – never shouting – but just constant, like he was fucking praying! Praying never to see me again.

And as soon as I walked out he slammed it shut.

–

Oh. Yeah. And when I showed up at my boyfriend's house in Brighton – he just – he said he felt sorry for me but this was all just a bit of fun and actually he wasn't looking for any drama so he didn't really feel comfortable letting me stay.

After I'd ripped my world apart for him.

–

Fuck that prick.

–

That was five days ago.

So. Thank you for letting me stay.

ALAN. In the spare room.

JOSH. It's somewhere.

> (**JOSH**'s *phone beeps. Ignores it.*)

ALAN. No. Well.

> (*Hug.*)

JOSH. Yeah.

You're getting better at this.

ALAN. Look. You can stay as long as you like. Honestly.

JOSH. -

ALAN. It's okay.

JOSH. Thank you.

ALAN. Don't mention it.

JOSH. No.

Thank you.

You should eat.

Your house really is incredible, by the way.

ALAN. Thanks.

JOSH. It's like Harry Potter should live here.

ALAN. I've not read it.

JOSH. What about the movies?

ALAN. No.

JOSH. How have you not seen Harry Potter?!

ALAN. I'm nearly forty.

JOSH. Mate, we gotta get you to watch those movies!

ALAN. I'm not sure they're for me?

JOSH. Not enough bats in them?

(The landline rings.)

ALAN. Christ! Did you put the phone on the hook?

JOSH. It was lying on the table – should I not?

ALAN. I don't like phone calls. If people need me they can email.

JOSH. Right.

(The ringing ends.)

ALAN. Phone calls are awful. Like people expect you to drop everything to talk to them. And they want to know things immediately. They don't give you the space to think.

JOSH. You should open that letter.

ALAN. It can wait.

JOSH. I saw the others. The pile on the kitchen table.

ALAN. Made yourself at home.

JOSH. They looked important.

They're going to take your home.

ALAN. Honestly, Josh –

JOSH. They can't do that.

ALAN. There's a new bit of dual carriageway. I live in the way. There's nothing I can do about it.

JOSH. Yes there is!

ALAN. Compulsory purchase means compulsory purchase.

JOSH. Bullshit, there must be something – my brother studies law, you can ask him –

ALAN. Are you even on speaking terms?

JOSH. Seriously Alan –

ALAN. Please. I don't want to talk about it.

JOSH. Have you answered any of their letters?

Mate.

Alan!

ALAN. You don't have any breakfast. You need to eat.

>*(The phone rings.* **JOSH** *looks at* **ALAN.** **JOSH** *reaches for it.* **ALAN** *holds his hand to stop him. It rings and rings. They stare at each other.)*
>
>*(It stops.)*
>
>(**JOSH***'s phone beeps. They stare at each other.)*
>
>(**ALAN** *lifts the receiver and leaves it off the hook.)*
>
>(**JOSH***'s phone beeps. And again.)*

Are you going to answer that?

–

Please. Let's just – get through today. Let's do something.

(The tunnel.)

ALAN. Mind your step.

JOSH. Entering the Chamber of Secrets.

That's another Harry Potter thing.

ALAN. Is it? Okay.

JOSH. So you're like his guardian.

ALAN. I suppose so. There's a few of us.

JOSH. But it's mainly you.

ALAN. Mainly. The local council do the bare minimum, even with all the endangered ones –Natterer's, Daubenton's, Bechstein's. They just chuck up the occasional bat bridge and think that's enough.

JOSH. Bat bridge?

ALAN. You see them over motorways. They are – if you'll excuse me – a load of bollocks. Bats don't use them.

Anyway.

There he is.

JOSH. Where?

ALAN. There. The pink – in the gap there, between those two bricks.

JOSH. Oh yeah.

He's – a bat.

ALAN. What were you expecting?

JOSH. Something bigger maybe.

ALAN. Wingspan of half a meter, he's the biggest bat in Britain.

JOSH. Well. Size isn't everything, innit?

You're really into him, eh?

ALAN. It's incredible, every time I see him.

I remember the first time – Tony showed me – Tony's the man who discovered him in the first place.

It wasn't long after they'd first found him and – it was like Christmas Day. Knowing I was about to see him, as Tony led me into the dark – I was nervous! Marching us along the tunnel, I could hear my heart beating so loud, I was worried they'd all hear it.

And there he was.

Seeing him – seeing the torchlight hit him and knowing he was – such a special –

I know, it's just a bat –

JOSH. No, I get it.

ALAN. Here for a few months every year and then gone. Like a rare flower.

JOSH. Where does he go?

ALAN. Maybe to France – fleeing to the continent for the summer months.

JOSH. On his holidays.

ALAN. But then he comes home to Britain.

JOSH. Is it his home though? If the rest of his species is in Europe?

ALAN. This is where he hibernates. It's the place where he feels safe. That's a home. Even if we drove the rest of them away.

JOSH. And he's the only one?

ALAN. Yes.

JOSH. Poor fucker.

ALAN. There was a bit of excitement in 2001, because someone found an elderly female greater mouse-eared bat in the roof of a cottage in Bognor Regis.

JOSH. Could they not get them to shag?

ALAN. Actually, the cottage burnt down.

What a horrible way to die.

JOSH. In a fire?

ALAN. In Bognor Regis.

JOSH. Lonely life.

ALAN. Very. They're meant to have several mates.

JOSH. Really?

ALAN. Yes. He should have a harem of females. That's the usual pattern for greater mouse-eareds.

JOSH. Would you like that?

ALAN. What?

JOSH. A harem.

ALAN. Oh no. I can barely handle myself – a harem would be overwhelming.

JOSH. D'you think?

ALAN. Don't you?

JOSH. The more the merrier, mate.

My ex and me – those first months at uni – we had so much sex. And one night we went back to one of his mates for a party, ended up in a massive orgy. Like, ten guys – all of them super fit too – it was so hot. One of the best nights of my life.

ALAN. Sounds – yes.

JOSH. You've never done that? Had a threesome? Or group sex?

ALAN. Is it important?

JOSH. No.

Maybe.

I make you feel awkward.

ALAN. I don't – not many people I know talk about sex. Really.

JOSH. I like it.

ALAN. What?

JOSH. Making you wriggle. Pulling you out of your comfort zone.

ALAN. I don't think I have a comfort zone.

JOSH. I think this is it, right here.

You're like – alive when you talk about it. It's sexy to be into something as much as you are.

ALAN. I don't – sexy isn't really –

JOSH. Fucking take the compliment, mate.

ALAN. Okay.

You're so much more comfortable with that – stuff.

JOSH. What? Being human?

ALAN. Huh. Silly boy.

JOSH. Serious man.

You're just as human as me.

ALAN. I'm just used to – myself.

JOSH. Well. Now you've got someone to look after you.

Let's go shopping. I'm going to "Queer Eye" you –

ALAN. I don't know what that –

JOSH. I know.

(Shopping.)

JOSH. They suit you!

ALAN. I have never worn a leather anything

JOSH. It looks great on you! Honestly –

ALAN. Do you think?

JOSH. Really! You're treating me, treat yourself too!

ALAN. If you're sure.

JOSH. You look so good, I could rip it off right here.

ALAN. Don't

–

–

OK, quick.

(Smoking.)

JOSH. Your first time – how's it feel?

ALAN. Well, how does it make one feel?

JOSH. How does it make YOU feel?

ALAN. How is it meant to make me feel?

JOSH. How do you feel now.

ALAN. I'm not sure I feel anything.

JOSH. You definitely feel something.

ALAN. No, I think I literally feel nothing.

JOSH. No feelings at all?

ALAN. Is orange a feeling?

(Eating.)

JOSH. I ordered us pizza.

ALAN. I was going to cook.

JOSH. Large pepperoni, stuffed crust, that OK?

ALAN. I'm sure it will be.

I suppose I'm a pizza person now.

JOSH. We're all pizza people, Alan.

ALAN. How life affirming to try new things.

JOSH. It's just Domino's mate, it's not the philosopher's stone.

ALAN. What?

JOSH. Alright, enough.

> *(Watching a movie.)*

ALAN. That was quite good.

JOSH. I told you.

ALAN. Is that it then? Voldemort's dead now?

JOSH. No no, there's seven more of them!

ALAN. Seven!

JOSH. Yep. Can I download the next one?

ALAN. Go on.

Alan Rickman is a very good baddie, isn't he?

JOSH. Just you wait.

> *(Post-shag.)*

ALAN. Good lord, that was – really – really good.

JOSH. Yeah.

–

The past few days have – you know?

Thank you.

ALAN. Thank you.

It's scary. But exciting.

JOSH. Still scared of me. Boo!

ALAN. Of most people.

JOSH. But not bats.

ALAN. Actually, I used to be scared of them.

JOSH. You're kidding?

ALAN. I was.

JOSH. Hahahahahahaha.

Seriously?

Hahahahaha.

ALAN. Why is that funny?

JOSH. I mean, cos you can't get enough of the little bastards now!

ALAN. I blame my uncle David. He came over one Christmas and insisted on watching an old Dracula film, a Christopher Lee one. I was only seven. So I didn't like bats for the longest time. Halloween was awful. I was convinced bats would snatch me up and deliver me to Dracula so he could suck me dry.

JOSH. So what changed?

ALAN. I was twelve. And our teacher announced we were going on a school trip the following week and to get our parents' permission. We were going to Arundel Castle in the morning –

JOSH. I've been there, it's wicked!

ALAN. Yeah, right? And then we were going to a bat hospital in the afternoon.

JOSH. They've got bat hospitals? That's adorable.

ALAN. I begged my parents not to let me go. My dad smacked me for crying and being a little pansy, and my mum just didn't –

anyway.

God, I haven't talked about this stuff in –

ever.

JOSH. That's fine.

ALAN. So I had to go to the bat hospital with everyone else. And I was shaking in the bus and one guy, Darren, was just singing the Batman theme tune the whole way – "dana nana nana nana, dana nana nana nana BATMAN" – and everyone thought he was hilarious.

And we got to this nice house in the country with a big garden and a pond and trees. And this lady came to meet us off the bus and said "hello boys and girls, my name is Jenny. Welcome to my home".

Her name is Jenny Clark – she's incredible – and when she took out an injured bat to show us – a noctule, quite large – she walked right up to me and – his furry body. Little sweet face. Bright eyes.

Just a patient in a hospital. Looking at me looking at him. And she showed me how to touch him and – I just stopped being scared.

People think they're scary, cos they go out at night. They fly. They're odd.

But people are odd too. It's just another creature trying to survive.

JOSH. Faced your fears, eh?

ALAN. Yes.

My parents didn't ever let me have a pet.

It's nice to have things to care for.

JOSH. You parents sound like – hard going.

ALAN. My dad was. I don't like football – he was a big Brighton fan. I don't like boxing – he'd been a county champion. I didn't like drinking – he was at the pub every night. I don't like – well – I didn't show any interest in girls –

JOSH. Just bats.

ALAN. Ha.

JOSH. What about your mum?

ALAN. She –

had a lot of problems.

–

She killed herself.

JOSH. Oh man.

ALAN. Yeah.

I hadn't seen her much – since they separated. She didn't want to see me anyway. She was – she struggled with living. A lot more than I do.

JOSH. You're doing pretty well, I think.

ALAN. I'm doing OK. Yeah.

–

(Kiss.)

Can we talk about you?

JOSH. I don't need it so much.

ALAN. No! I'm interested.

JOSH. It's late.

ALAN. You can leave if you want to.

JOSH. Why would I want to?

ALAN. Look at us – honestly – look at you and then look at me!

JOSH. What the fuck are you talking about?

ALAN. Why would you want to be with me?

(Breaths.)

JOSH. Cos you're the kinda guy who asks that question.

–

I'm gonna shower.

ALAN. Will you sleep in here tonight?

JOSH. – OK

ALAN. I like looking after you.

JOSH. Another little bat. Squeak squeak.

ALAN. No. I like you because you're you.

(Sunset. A hillside.)

JOSH. The sunset never looks like that.

ALAN. It does here.

JOSH. Those colours – like – you know in school when you'd dip a paintbrush in a jar of water? Bleeding yellow and orange and red streaks – beautiful.

ALAN. I like stopping up here. On my way home. One can breathe.

(Breaths.)

*(**JOSH**'s phone beeps. He looks – pockets it.)*

JOSH. I can see your house.

ALAN. Yes.

JOSH. Have you always lived there?

ALAN. It's been my family's for a hundred and fifty years.

JOSH. Wow –

ALAN. It's a bit –

JOSH. Compared to our semi-d, it's a fucking palace mate.

ALAN. Yes – sorry.

It's too big for me though. My great-grandparents had seven children. They needed all the room.

He was a grain merchant – and an MP, actually. Briefly.

JOSH. Lah-di-dah.

ALAN. My granddad lost a lot of the family business in a banking thing, ended up running a removals company. Dad kept that going, and a taxi firm. Got done for drink driving so that wasn't a huge help. Only child – so it came down to me.

The glory days are behind it. Nothing but former greatness.

JOSH. Oh I think you're pretty great. Saving the world, one bat at a time.

ALAN. It's nothing in the greater scheme though really, is it?

JOSH. It's everything.

He needs a name. By the way. We can't just keep calling him "The Bat".

Jeff. Jeff The Bat.

ALAN. Really?

JOSH. I know, you're a very serious person. It should be Jeffrey.

ALAN. You don't know him very well. I think you should call him Mister Bat for now.

JOSH. That was almost a joke, Alan.

ALAN. Almost.

JOSH. And I know you don't like it. But I think being Batman is cool.

Not all heroes wear capes.

If it helps, you can call me Robin. Your little orphan sidekick. The Boy Wonder.

ALAN. Is that Harry Potter again?

JOSH. That's The Boy Who Lived.

ALAN. - Aren't all boys the boy who lived?

JOSH. Oh my days, you're so uneducated.

ALAN. You're so young.

JOSH. Don't do that.

ALAN. What?

JOSH. I'm not a child –

ALAN. I'm not saying that.

JOSH. I know what people mean when they say "you're so young". They mean you don't know what you're saying, you don't have experience, you don't understand – I've got a lot more experience than you, man –

ALAN. I know –

JOSH. I've lived.

ALAN. I know, I know –

JOSH. Saying that puts distance between us. Don't do that. I'm as old as you in lots of ways.

ALAN. I know.

I just mean that – you've got so much time.

JOSH. Well. So do you. Plenty of time.

(Holding him.)

ALAN. Alright.

JOSH. How old is Jeff?

ALAN. Sixteen.

JOSH. Is that old?

ALAN. *Myotis myotis* has been known to live past thirty.

JOSH. So he's middle-aged?

ALAN. I hate that, middle-aged.

JOSH. And I hate being called young.

ALAN. It's sad.

JOSH. Is it?

ALAN. Middle-aged? Yes. It means there's a point when suddenly you go from having more of your life ahead of you to having more of it behind you. There's a tipping point when you stop counting up and start counting down.

JOSH. You could just keep counting up.

You never know the middle point anyway. Maybe you ain't reached it.

ALAN. Or it's well in the past.

JOSH. What if I've reached mine?

ALAN. You haven't.

JOSH. I could be ninety percent done.

ALAN. Statistically very unlikely.

JOSH. Who knows how long anyone has?

ALAN. There's –

This isn't really – science – really. It's very inexact. But –

So there's a theory that we all have a finite number of heartbeats. We all have a billion heartbeats to live. Humans, cats, dogs, rats – all our hearts beat at different speeds but we all have the same amount. A clock with a billion ticks.

JOSH. That doesn't sound right.

ALAN. Like I said – it's not exact.

JOSH. It sounds like ages. If we live for, say, eighty years? Is that really a billion heartbeats? Cos like – a billion heartbeats – that sounds like forever.

ALAN. That's a life. Eighty years for humans. Ten or twelve years for a dog. A year or two for a mouse. Many more for a whale. Though actually – here's the funny thing

– humans are longer lived for their size than they should be.

JOSH. What you mean?

ALAN. So – if you imagine a graph, like *(Drawing in the air.)* lifespan and then size of animal, the line goes up at a pretty similar rate to how it goes forward. The bigger the animal, the slower their heart beats so *(Tracing an imaginary curve.)* the bigger they are, the longer they live. But humans are ahead of the curve. And so are bats. Of the mammals who are longest lived by size, humans are the tops and the rest of the top twenty is pretty much all bats. Such little creatures, and they just keep on living. Longer than they ever should.

JOSH. Maybe it's cos they're lonely. Maybe they never meet someone who makes their heart beat a little faster. Maybe I'm taking years off your life.

Ba-dum ba-dum ba-dum ba-dum ba-dum ba-dum –

ALAN. Who says you do that?

JOSH. You're right Alan. It's a steep hill – maybe that's what raised your pulse. Shortened your breath. Turned your cheeks red – you're blushing!

ALAN. I'm not.

–

JOSH. We're going to save it. Your house.

ALAN. I'll have money, I'll find somewhere else –

JOSH. No. That's your home. Your history is there. Tomorrow we're going to march into the council offices and we're going to demand to – see – someone.

ALAN. Ha. Excellent plan.

–

I love you.

(Some silence. And some more.)

JOSH. Have you ever said that before?

ALAN. No.

It's only been a few days. I know. But you're the person who made me want to say it.

You don't have to say it back.

JOSH. -

Alright.

-

-

ALAN. Alright.

NEWSREADER. Local environmental groups continue to protest the imminent Chichester bypass project. Patricia Bramwell from Conservation Sussex had this to say.

PATRICIA BRAMWELL. This will have a devastating impact on countless endangered species of wildlife and flora. There hasn't been sufficient local consultation, in our eyes. We will be protesting this every step of the way.

(The morning after. **JOSH** *holding* **ALAN**'s *wallet.)*

ALAN. Where are you going?

JOSH. Fuck. I thought you were still asleep.

ALAN. I woke up. Are you going out for breakfast?

JOSH. Yes.

–

ALAN. Are you leaving?

JOSH. –

Yes.

ALAN. Is it because I said –

JOSH. No.

Nothing, you did nothing.

ALAN. It is. I ruined it –

JOSH. You didn't!

–

My family know where I am.

ALAN. How do you know?

JOSH. My brother texted. They figured out the password for my computer and checked Find My iPhone. They can see exactly where I am, they're coming here if I don't come home. I can't stay.

ALAN. You said they kicked you out.

JOSH. And now they want to – bring me back. They said they've prayed about it.

ALAN. You're an adult, they don't own you, they can't just drag you out of here –

JOSH. Yes they can.

ALAN. I won't let them.

JOSH. You can't stop them.

ALAN. They're just people.

JOSH. You hate people.

ALAN. I love you. I don't want you to go.

JOSH. You don't need all my problems –

ALAN. You're not a problem –

JOSH. Another letter arrived. The purchase is going through next week.

–

I think you need one less problem in your life.

ALAN. You're not a problem Josh!

JOSH. Well I'm not a fucking solution! Staying here ain't going to solve anything.

ALAN. Then I'll come with you.

JOSH. You mad?

ALAN. No. I mean it. You said yourself, next week I won't have this place anyway. Neither of us have anywhere to go so let's go nowhere together. Isn't that a good idea? Isn't it?

JOSH. No. This is your home.

ALAN. Not for much longer.

JOSH. I told you, you can appeal! Don't just roll over for them!

ALAN. I don't want to live here –

JOSH. A hundred and fifty years of history!

ALAN. Who wants all those ghosts for housemates?

I just want you.

I love you Josh.

JOSH. Stop saying that!

ALAN. Why? If now isn't the time to say it then when is?

If not to you, then to whom?

JOSH. You don't love me!

ALAN. I wouldn't lie to you!

–

Were you stealing my wallet?

You could have just asked, Josh.

JOSH. You don't know me.

ALAN. Yes I do – I'd give you the world. A week ago I was nothing and now – I would actually share this life with you. If you'd let me.

JOSH. Grindr will find me a bed.

ALAN. You can't disappear. Not now I've found you.

(*JOSH's phone beeps.*)

JOSH. Urrrggghhhhhhh.

Shittttt.

–

Fucking hell man.

ALAN. I'm going to brush my teeth, pack a bag, grab my phone and we can go. Together.

Alright?

This is maybe the first time I've decided to do anything, ever. You can't change my mind.

JOSH. Shit.

Alright.

ALAN. Excellent.

>*(He kisses **JOSH**.)*

I'll be five minutes.

>*(**JOSH** waits. He pulls his phone out of his pocket, leaves it with **ALAN**'s wallet. He goes to leave. He lingers. He looks up at the ceiling. He grabs the wallet again. Almost doesn't leave. Leaves.)*

ALAN. The common vampire bat is one of three solely sanguivorous – blood consuming – vampire bats in the world. They're the only ones which feed primarily on mammals – including, albeit rarely, on humans. A vampire bat won't swoop down on its prey. Instead, it lands and approaches carefully on the ground, often while their target is asleep. It locates a warm spot on the skin – a weak point – where it makes a small incision with their razor-sharp teeth. They don't suck the blood, but instead lap it up, drinking their fill, rapidly absorbing, digesting and urinating as they take full advantage of their unwitting blood donor. They are so perfectly equipped for their task, their saliva even prevents their victim's blood from clotting, prolonging bleeding. They are so masterful, their victim may not even be aware they are being preyed upon.

(The tunnel.)

*(**ALAN** shines his torch at the roof of the cave.)*

(Another torch flares on.)

JOSH. I'm making a citizen's arrest!

ALAN. Jesus!

JOSH. Hello, stranger.

Do you come here often?

ALAN. You –

JOSH. I'm sorry.

ALAN. Sorry isn't good enough –

JOSH. I didn't know what to do –

ALAN. He's gone.

JOSH. What?

ALAN. The greater mouse-eared bat. He's gone.

JOSH. Really?

ALAN. Didn't you think to check?

JOSH. / No?

ALAN. / No, because you don't care –

JOSH. I didn't think / to –

ALAN. / Do you ever?

–

You did this.

JOSH. No.

ALAN. You drove him away.

JOSH. I didn't.

ALAN. This is what you do is it? Tear my life into a million pieces – and this is the final piece.

JOSH. I didn't –

ALAN. Have you been sleeping here?

JOSH. The last couple of nights, yes –

ALAN. There you go. Waking a bat from hibernation can kill them –

JOSH. Maybe he woke up naturally –

ALAN. It's still January!

Well done. You've just killed the last of his kind in this country. Congratulations.

JOSH. I didn't mean –

ALAN. What do you mean?

Hmm?

Do you mean anything? At all?

Do you have any grand plan? Or is your existence just one stream of unintended fucking consequences?

–

The police came, the day you left.

They told me what happened.

You stole from your parents.

(Breaths.)

JOSH. Alan –

ALAN. The story about your boyfriend – a lie?

A sob story.

You're just a thief.

–

–

Does he even exist?

–

Do they even know? That you're gay.

JOSH. No.

I can't tell them.

ALAN. Huh.

–

They're worried.

JOSH. Did you tell them –?

ALAN. I met you in the pub, you were tired and emotional. You stayed a couple nights and took off with no explanation.

JOSH. Thank you.

ALAN. It's only the truth, I didn't do it for you.

(Breaths.)

JOSH. Fucking –

–

I'm sorry.

ALAN. Liar.

Liar liar liar liar liar liar / liar –

JOSH. / I am.

ALAN. I don't believe you.

JOSH. You shouldn't. I know. Cos I'm a cunt – I know you wouldn't say it but –

ALAN. You're a cunt –

JOSH. –

I don't deserve your help or your love –

shit!

Please don't look at me right now, please.

–

When you said that, the other day – that you love me – it fucking – I couldn't let you say that. I don't deserve that or you or anything cos I'm a fucking piece of shit. I had to get out –

ALAN. I appreciate the favour.

JOSH. No no no, I fucking know man – I know, fuck knows I know what a cunt I am.

–

I don't want to – I just need to – explain – and you can fucking –

So this is who I am, OK?

I don't know what I want. I'm – I'm not special.

I'm never going to be – so I fucking – I decided, whatever they want me to be, that's what I'm not. I wanted to sin, alright? Just little things – sweets from the shop, cans, whatever – shit from my mates – and then bigger things, cash from my parents' wallets –

– a ring from my granny's bedside table –

I sold it.

I just did it. I didn't even need anything, I just bought some sunglasses –

And then my granny died. Mum wanted to bury her with the ring on – and when she couldn't find it – I told her she'd probably lost it. Or given it away – she went a bit crazy at the end –

and then – mum caught me taking money from the collection box in the church. That shit goes to – like, homeless people, sick kids, people who actually fucking need –

and she realised immediately, about the ring.

I couldn't – her face – I just fucking ran. I just –

I can't even – think –

–

–

I'm so much worse than you realised.

ALAN. You are.

JOSH. You should hate me.

ALAN. I should.

JOSH. What if I did kill him? Jeff. What if I threw stones at him and knocked him off the wall and stamped up and down on him so his guts spewed out and his eyes burst in his head and his blood sprayed everywhere, hmm? Stamping him to death shouting FUCK THIS BAT AND FUCK THIS WORLD AND FUCK YOU AND FUCK EVERYTHING!

(Breaths.)

ALAN. I've just realised. You get prettier when you lie. That's how you do it. You lie yourself pretty.

JOSH. You just –

why won't you hate me?

ALAN. It's too late, isn't it?

JOSH. It would be easier if you did.

ALAN. I agree.

–

You lied about something else.

You said you were killing me – taking years off my life. But don't they also say, when you fall in love your heart skips a beat? So actually you earn a few extra moments between now and a billion heartbeats. You gain time.

So. That's why I never said I love you to anyone, before. Because when it inevitably falls apart – as it has –

–

it means all I've actually done is just gained a little bit more of a god-awful lonely life.

Don't love. Don't hate. Just – nothing.

It's a hell of a lot easier if people don't matter. And a hell of lot quicker.

–

I nearly said it to another boy once. I was your age. But I couldn't bear the thought of everything that would follow. I was better off just – not.

–

Opening that door is so –

–

JOSH. Doesn't mean you shouldn't open it.

ALAN. Hypocrite. Liar and hypocrite.

I was doing fine until you arrived –

JOSH. Were you?

ALAN. I was surviving –

JOSH. Surviving isn't living. Your heart needs to swell, and break, and – man – it's everything –

ALAN. Look at you. Hiding in the dark.

You're as bad as me.

–

May I have my phone back?

You did take it, didn't you?

–

JOSH. -

A nurse rang a few times.

Over the last few days.

Your mum wants you to call.

–

(Breaths.)

ALAN. She's in a home. She had a stroke, ten years ago. I never visit. Why would I?

We never – you know?

I just say she's dead. It's easier.

I don't know why I said she killed herself.

(Breaths.)

What do I do?

JOSH. Something else.

ALAN. What a stupid life –

JOSH. It's not stupid –

ALAN. All those years on something fucking – worthless –

JOSH. You don't believe that.

You found the thing you loved and gave it everything –

ALAN. I didn't do anything!

JOSH. You cared. It's your thing.

ALAN. And you lie. It's your thing.

JOSH. Everybody lies. It's how we make people care.

    (Breaths.)

ALAN. Two runaways.

JOSH. We're all just running, ain't we?

Maybe that's what Jeff did.

Or maybe he met someone.

ALAN. Why did you come back here?

JOSH. I couldn't think of anywhere else –

–

You?

–

Did you think I'd be here?

ALAN. Probably.

    *(**JOSH** collapses.)*

    *(**ALAN** sits. Holds him.)*

    *(**JOSH** holds him back.)*

    (They move apart. Hands almost touching but not.)

    (A news report.)

NEWSREADER. Ground was broken today on the new Chichester Bypass amidst a hail of protests from environmental groups. Chichester council cabinet member George Topping said that their concerns had been taken into consideration.

GEORGE TOPPING. This is going to be one of the greenest roads ever constructed. For example, we've ring-fenced three hundred thousand pounds to construct two bat bridges along bat hunting routes. We will all, ultimately, be very proud of this project which secures a brighter, happier future for all concerned.

> (**ALAN** *looks to the ceiling.* **JOSH** *looks at* **ALAN**. *Sounds of squeaking and flittering.*)
>
> *(Louder.)*
>
> *(Louder.)*
>
> *(Blackout.)*

End

ABOUT THE AUTHOR

Barry McStay is an Irish writer and actor based in London. *Vespertilio* is his UK debut play, winning a Show of the Week Award at VAULT Festival in February 2019. It later ran at Smock Alley at the Dublin Fringe Festival in September 2019 before being filmed for streaming by the King's Head Theatre in April 2021.

His first play *Our Island* ran at the Dublin Fringe Festival 2015 and was nominated for five Dublin Fringe Awards and a Writers Guild of Ireland Award. Other work includes *Bir Tawil* and *The First*.

He has written short work for Miniaturists and the Abbey Theatre. In 2018, he was one of thirty writers selected to create a play for *A Play For Ireland* by Fishamble: The New Play Company. His writing has been longlisted for the Bruntwood Prize, the Theatre503 Playwriting Award and the Papatango Prize.

Barry has a BA (English Literature & History) from Trinity College Dublin and an MA (Acting) from East 15 Acting School.

Lightning Source UK Ltd.
Milton Keynes UK
UKHW011605160421
382087UK00009B/559